eBay Selling Mastery

How to make $5000 per Month Selling Stuff on eBay

Table of Content

Introduction

I want to thank you and congratulate you for downloading the book, eBay Mastery.

This book is for those of you who are new to selling on eBay. It contains proven steps and strategies on how to start making money now by selling various types of items on eBay.

Whether you just want to sell off some stuff from your attic or whether you aim to start your own business, there's money to be made selling items on eBay. In this volume I'll show you how to get started, how to prepare your eBay listing, and how to begin making a profit. There's a lot of money exchanging hands on eBay. Why shouldn't some of it end up in your pocket?

Thanks again for downloading this book, I hope you enjoy it!

Chapter 1 – How to get started selling on Ebay

Back in 1995, a man named Pierre Omidyar created the computer code for an auction web site that he called AuctionWeb. To test out his program, he put a 'test item' up for bidding---a broken laser pointer. Much to his surprise, people bid on it! Omidyar contacted the winning bidder, reminding him that it was a *broken* laser pointer. Guess what? The bidder replied that he was a collector of broken laser pointers!

So AuctionWeb became eBay, and it grew and grew. It finally went public in 1998... and a new way of buying and selling was born. eBay has expanded to more than two dozen countries since its modest beginnings, and it's become more than a forum for selling unwanted things from around the house. That's a lot of buying and selling...and you can be part of it if you're willing to invest some time and effort. How to get started? Read on.

First, you need to browse the web site, maybe bid on a few items, especially if you're not familiar with how it works. Second, you need to make some sort of plan. Just what are you thinking of selling? The various chapters in this book can help you with that decision. There are a number of different approaches, as you will see, and one of them will be just right for you. Third, you need to set up some accounts and get a feedback rating before you list anything for sale. The ins and outs of creating the listing that will actually sell your product will be covered in the final chapter.

Obviously, you need to create an eBay account to become a seller there. It's free and easy. The second item you need is a PayPal account (also free and easy). If you already have a PayPal account, you'll need to upgrade it to a Premier account so you can receive money and accept credit cards when selling on eBay. You guessed it, free and easy! Buyers really prefer using PayPal and some won't consider buying without it, so set up that account. Although there's sometimes a temporary hold put on funds, PayPal can offer you a great deal of protection as a seller. You can also avoid dealing with personal checks (very iffy!) by having the buyer send it through PayPal from his/her bank account via an e-check.

Once those things are accomplished there's one last thing you need to do before settling down to sell. You need a feedback score. Unfortunately it's not free, but it is easy. If you've bought things on eBay, you already have a feedback score from the people you bought from. Check it out and make sure it looks good. You need at least five (ten is better) feedback ratings. If you haven't bought anything through eBay, you need to do it now. It's your reputation on the site, and without it you will have a very hard time attracting reputable buyers, which are the ones you want. Right?

The cost of the items you purchase to establish your feedback score doesn't matter---only the number of separate purchases. One great way to kill two birds with one stone is to buy things that you'll need for packing and/or shipping what you plan to sell or buy the things that you'll need to run a home business if you plan to 'go big' with selling. Packing materials, padded envelopes, printing labels are all available, as are printers, computers, desks, and software. You can also buy everyday items on eBay, like toothpaste, or gift items for future family birthdays. So take care of some shopping while you build your feedback.

Once you've got your accounts and feedback in order, you're ready to start planning what you're going to sell and how you're going to make money on eBay. The possibilities range from wholesale novelty items to drop shipping, from product flipping to working a specialized niche, and from breaking up bundles to selling nothing at all. Confused? Don't be. These will all be explained in the following chapters, and you'll find the eBay spot that suits you to a T.

Chapter 2 – What to sell, and what not to sell on Ebay

Your 'stuff' may be the reason you're thinking about selling things on eBay in the first place. Many people have attics, basements, and garages full of 'stuff' they'd like to clear out. Unfortunately, many of those items will not sell well on eBay and you'll waste your time and money listing them. [Yes, there *is* a cost involved in selling items on eBay. It's reasonably low, but it's a cost nonetheless.] There are also some surprising things that *will* actually sell. Remember the original 'test item', a broken laser pointer? It sold for $15! So, while it's true that you can sell anything on eBay, you might wait a long time before the right buyer comes along. It's best to avoid the hard items when you're getting started.

So, what doesn't sell well? Jewelry usually doesn't, especially good jewelry. On eBay buyers have to really trust that you're telling the truth about it's being real. Really now, would you buy it yourself? You're better off selling jewelry locally, where people can actually see it and have it appraised if they want to. Antiques are the same, plus they involve enormous shipping fees and awkward packaging.

Books, comics, and vinyl LP's are only worth something if they're rare, special in some way, and/or in excellent condition. These items fall into a 'collectors' category that requires a lot of research. Without really knowing what you've got, you'll risk either wasting your time or getting ripped off. If you run across some old books or records that you think may be worth something, have them appraised locally before listing them on eBay. If you live near a university, however, reselling current popular textbooks can be a great business.

Clothing is another 'iffy' category. Brand new *with tags and brand name* will sell. Otherwise, it may sit around forever. Again, of course, there are specialty items, like bridal gowns, that will move well if they're priced right, and vintage clothing. Selling clothes on eBay takes a lot of research and you'll need to put in the time to learn the tricks involved in creating listings that get good bids. The same is true for anything homemade, no matter how nice it is. Sometimes creating an eBay store is best for these kinds of items.

However, many broken items can be sold if you price them right or if they're rare/old. There are a lot of folks out there who'll buy it cheap and repair it. This is especially true of household and yard stuff like weed-eaters and toasters, or older items like 1950's electric razors. Again, you'll need to do some research.

How do you some of that research? First see if anything similar has sold on eBay and what it sold for. eBay actually makes this easy, too. Here's how: log in and use the search box in the upper right-hand corner of the home page to search for your item. This will give you a list of the current auctions, and you don't want that right now. To the left, you'll see a group of boxes where you can tick off categories. Check 'completed listings', then hit 'search' again. This will give you a list of all the closed auctions, in other words a list of the items that actually sold. If the price is in <u>red</u>, that item <u>didn't sell</u>. You're looking for the *green* prices. You'll be able to get a good idea of the market value of your item, as well as how that particular item compares to yours as far as size, condition, or whatever. Searching the completed auctions is something you will use again and again for researching different things.

So, that's 'your stuff', but what's the 'small stuff'? A lot of people make very good money on eBay selling small items in volume. Novelty items, like Groucho Marx glasses, can be bought wholesale for ridiculously low prices and resold individually for an astounding profit. Key chains, cheap toys, all the stuff you can pick up in a dollar store, you can purchase in bulk and sell individually. Also many household items [did you buy that toothpaste on eBay earlier for feedback?] can be handled the same way. If you live in an area that has a specialty item of its own---something you can get easily but that is not sold nationally---you can sell that. Selling the 'small stuff' requires that you list a number of different items at the same time, usually in the Marketplace, if you plan to make money, and, of course, you'll need to be able to store it all somewhere. And if packing all that little stuff for shipment is a pain, hire some local kids to stuff those Groucho Marx specs in the envelopes. They'll work cheap, particularly if you give them a free pair! Check out some of the novelty items on eBay, do the math, and you'll see that these sellers are making a large profit!

Bundles...ah, bundles. Bundles are a way of acquiring stock to sell as well as a way of selling small items. Bundles, sometimes known as 'lots', are simply a number of items that are all being sold as one item. Many people find a collection of porcelain frogs in a box in the attic and list it on eBay as 'Porcelain Frog Collection'. That's a bundle. Those little froggies may actually sell for much more when sold individually than the price that's being asked for the collection. So you buy them (do some research in case some may be really valuable) and list them separately. Browse the listings and you'll find tools, comic books, video games, and many other items being sold this way. If you've ever watched 'Storage Wars' on TV, you'll understand the principle right away. There are eBay sellers who specialize in buying bundles and re-listing each item separately.

Conversely, if you get into selling the 'small stuff', you can list bundles to increase your profit on the items. If novelty toys are your thing, then put together a piñata bundle or a children's party bundle or a gag gift collection. You'll be able to get a little more per item that way. You can do the same with any small, low-priced stuff. It just takes a little time and imagination.

Chapter 3 - Hobby & Niche Items

A hobby can be a tremendous way to start selling on eBay. Your knowledge of that hobby and what supplies it requires can give you a starting point for what to sell. If something is hard to get in your town, it's probably hard for other hobbyists to get in their towns. So supply it! Many things are much less expensive purchased in bulk, but most of us can't ever store or use that much product. But you could sell that much...hmmm. Special sales are another source of hobby items; buy on sale, sell just below normal retail. And a 'going out of business' sale can be a gold mine! It doesn't matter what your hobby is, you and other hobbyists need something...instructions, books, or supplies. There's a market out there, so check out things for your hobby on eBay. Are the suppliers there asking too much? Is the quality low or the quantity awkward? Perhaps there isn't anyone selling good stuff for your particular hobby. If you can do better, then go for those hobby dollars and put your unique knowledge to work for you.

Niches in the market are another area where your special knowledge can give you an advantage. Just about anything collectible is a niche. From coins to vintage clothing, you need to know what you're dealing with and what has value. More importantly, you need to know what doesn't have any real market value. If you're a collector, or would like to become an expert in something, then the niche market is for you. Thrift shops, flea markets, and garage sales abound with items that are practically being given away, and many of those items have a good market with collectors.

How do you know if it's worth buying? You spy a Santa figurine in the thrift shop. Two dollars. It's in beautiful condition, but can you resell it for a profit? Your smart phone is your best on-the-go friend here. Use that search function on eBay for completed auctions. What have Santa figurines sold for? If you're lucky, you may find one just like the one you're looking at in the store. What did it sell for? Have smaller uglier ones sold for $15? Maybe it's a good buy---do some quick mental math, remembering listing fees, shipping, etc. You can make a decision on the spot. If you know your niche, you'll know a bargain when you see it.

Another way to work the niche market, without becoming an expert yourself, is to find out what people are looking for. Then buy it and resell it. In that search function on eBay, you can click on any completed auction. You'll see how many bids were placed for that one item ... and more importantly how many bidders. If there was a lot of interest, you can find that same item elsewhere. Use the Internet, the classifieds, or other auction sites. Someone somewhere is selling that thing for way below its value. Find it, buy it, and list it.

An interesting story of finding the right market for an item comes from a long time eBay seller referred to as King

Human (really). He happened on a stash of 3M thermal fax machines, long since out of production and obsolete. People will pay you to haul them out of their storerooms. But some research turned up the interesting fact that these machines were actually in demand, but not by the business community. Tattoo artists had found that these old outdated machines were perfect for creating their transfer patterns. He could sell these things like hotcakes in the tattooing market since they couldn't buy new ones anywhere. He found the right niche for selling those old fax machines and made handfuls of money.

Now don't run out looking for old fax machines. That's just an example, and maybe the tattoo industry has moved on. It simply serves to illustrate that old adage 'One man's junk is another man's treasure'. If you can find a market with a need, and you fill that need, you will be successful selling on eBay. Again, research, research, and research.

Chapter 4 - Flipping & Drop Shipping

You're familiar with the term flipping from all the house shows on TV, but flipping is an eBay activity as well. Just like on TV, flippers look for items that are selling way below value. They buy them and remarket them appropriately for a profit. There are a number of reasons that people don't bid on things at eBay, and flipping takes advantage of that. So if you like browsing the listings, flipping may be your avenue to making good money on eBay.

So why wouldn't there be any bids on an item? Of course, if it's a piece of junk no one is going to buy it. Flippers don't buy junk---not if profit is their goal and it is. One reason that a good item doesn't attract bidders is spelling...yes, spelling. If the title listing is misspelled, no one will find that item on search. If they don't find it, they can't bid on it. Spelling mistakes and typos are far more common than you'd think. A flipper would check out the possible misspellings to try to track down these items. [There are actually software programs that will do this, if you care to invest in one. Errors in spelling are really THAT common!] Then the flipper could buy with a low bid and resell at market price. Alternatively, they could contact the seller from a completed but unsuccessful auction to see if the item is still available. After failing to sell at auction, a lot of people will take a low price just to get rid of whatever it is. In either scenario, the item gets flipped.

Apart from misspelling, bad photos or bad descriptions will also turn potential buyers away from an auction. This is why creating a good listing is crucial to good sales, and the last chapter of this book will give you tips on how to create a great listing. Another reason that things are available below market price is that sometimes people don't know what they have. They think it's a kitchen spoon rest and it's really an art deco ashtray. Again, a little research would have gotten this item into the correct category and therefore in front of the people who want to buy it.

A final reason that things don't draw bids is that the potential buyers don't feel confidence or trust in the seller. They'll move on and perhaps even pay a little more to someone else. Sellers who want cash, checks, or money orders don't inspire confidence that they'll actually send (or even have) the item. Neither do sellers with no feedback rating or, worse, a bad feedback score. As a flipper you may be able to get that item, especially if you can arrange to pick it up in person, for a very low price. Then *your* PayPal account and *your* good feedback will put buyers' minds ate ease. Item flipped.

A variation on flipping is tailor made for those of you who are good at repairing things. Like the original 'test item', that broken laser pointer, there are many things for sale on eBay that are only partially functional, broken, or in bad condition. If you have the skills to bring them back to life, you can resell the refurbished item at a profit. Look for these items in your own skill area. You'll need to guesstimate the cost of repair to ensure you make a profit, but many things only need a quick fix by someone who knows how to be fully functional once again. You can also pick up stock for this in thrift shops or at garage sales. Buy it, fix it, and sell it on eBay. And remember, even cars and boats are sold on eBay.

Another way to make money on eBay is through drop shipping. This means that you're selling things that you don't actually have. You are the middleman between the buyer and the actual seller (and shipper). If you've ever bought something online and had it shipped directly to someone else, you've basically drop shipped. Many of the large items sold on eBay are actually sold through drop shipping, but many smaller or new items are as well.

Here's how it works. You win my auction and pay for the item. I then order the item from my drop shipper and give your name and address as the 'ship to'. They process the order and send the item directly to you. The difference between what you pay me and what I pay them is my profit. The obvious disadvantage is that I'm responsible and risk bad feedback if the drop shipper screws up or if the item is out of stock or backordered. I may have to refund your money, even if I don't get my money back from the shipper.

The other disadvantage is that you have to sign up with a drop shipper and open an account. With most, this means you need to pay a monthly membership charge. This enables you to get wholesale prices on things, which you then sell for closer to retail prices. You can still undersell most stores because you have no costs other than the drop shipper membership fee.

The big advantage to drop shipping is that you don't have to spend anything up front on inventory. When the customer orders, you order. You don't have to store or ship any merchandise at all. You can also sell a wide variety of different items, and you can sell larger or more expensive items such as pet doors or TV's that no one wants to have to pack up or lug around.

Drop shipping can also make it possible for you to sell specialty items that may not be available everywhere. You can create your own niche in the market. Smaller specialty businesses usually don't require a fee to serve as a drop shipper, but they may require you to submit an application. Your range of product will be much smaller than with the large companies but also more unique.

Many people run 'virtual' stores from their spare bedrooms by using drop shipping and selling on eBay. If you're really aiming to make a sizable monthly income as an eBay seller, then drop shipping has real possibilities for you. There are several major drop shippers with access to hundreds of wholesalers that you can find via the Internet but check them out well. Your reputation as an eBay merchant rests on their reliability.

Still not sure which way to go? Visit a web site called Terapeak.com. This site analyzes eBay sales and you can find out which items are selling the best in real time. There are two ways to use this information. One is to jump on the bandwagon and sell some of the very popular items. The other is to look at the listings for things that you'd think would sell well but they aren't. Can you figure out why? This kind of research can assist you in finding underserved or poorly served markets. Bingo ...a niche to fill.

Selling something you know about or care about can help you focus your efforts. It also serves to keep your determination strong. Your motivation, determination, knowledge, and effort will make you successful in the long run.

Marketing will also greatly increase your sales. Make a plan and follow through with it. Whether it's Facebook pages, blog posts, or offering discounts, you need to generate interest in what you're selling. Time, initiative, and creativity are all it takes. Oh, and research.

Chapter 5 – Making money without selling anything: the eBay Affiliate Program

Selling nothing? I can do that? Before you get too excited here, you should know that becoming an affiliate *does* involve having more computer skills than the other options. It is also a very lucrative option for those who can work it well. The eBay affiliate program is a referral service, basically. It involves setting up web sites with product links that send buyers to eBay. eBay pays you for each new user that registers and for each user that bids on (or buys) an item within 30 days. They also provide the banners, links, etc., that you need for your web sites. However, you need to be comfortable creating and maintaining multiple web sites to make this work for you. If this is not up your alley, move on to the next chapter on creating an eBay listing for an item. If you're experienced with web site creation, are willing to learn, or already have a web site, then read on.

The starting point to become an eBay affiliate is to sign up for an account. Look for 'eBay Affiliate Program' on their home page and fill out the application. You will also need to sign up for an account with Commission Junction. Both accounts are free. Be forewarned that eBay will reject your application if your web site promotes violence, illegal activities, sexually explicit materials, or discrimination of any kind. You also may not have 'eBay' (or any variation of it) in your domain name or be in violation of intellectual property rights. Once you're approved, you're ready to begin.

If you already have a web site, go to Commission Junction. After logging in, go to the Merchant Partner area and choose eBay. Towards the bottom of the page you'll find 'Show Links'. Click this; then choose the link you'd like and select 'Get HTML'. You'll copy and paste the HTML code to your own web page. Voila!

If you're setting up new web sites, follow the instructions and tutorials in your site builder program to get it up and running. You'll transfer the links in the same manner described above.

Most exclusively affiliate web sites are built for the niche market---pottery, vintage clothing, baby items, tools, etc. Since there are thousands of items that you can link to in eBay, you'll need to set up multiple sites catering to different segments of the market if you want to make serious money per month. You'll also need to attract buyers to your site with blogs, reviews, key words, and perhaps paid searches like Google AdWords. Information for doing all these things is readily available on the web. The more you learn, the more customers will shop eBay through your site ... and the more money you'll make.

Chapter 6 – How to List items on Ebay: step by step

Actually making your listing in eBay is very straightforward. Follow their instructions on the web site. It's easy to do and you can walk through it yourself. The question is really how to make a listing that sells.

There's tons of advice available on the Internet about the best way to list and sell on eBay... and tons of different opinions. Once you've decided what you're selling, you can look for special tips and tricks in that particular area of sales since different items do require different techniques. My aim here is to summarize the most common suggestions on listing and to keep it general.

Before you list:

- Research your item. Know what the market value is for *that item in that condition.*

- Take good photos and use a photo-editing program to improve them.

- Write a good and accurate description detailing positives and negatives. If it's chipped, say so. Bulleted lists are good for this.

- Choose your key words: what would you search for if you were looking for your item? Make sure your key words are in your description as well. there's a free tool to help with this, called eBay Pulse, that shows the current most popular search terms in each category.

- Write your listing title with care. Check spelling and include brand names.

- Prepare your listing in advance so you can review and fine-tune it. You can pay a little extra to do this on eBay or download eBay's free program Turbo-Lister. For multiple listings, go with Turbo-Lister. You can save partial listings, add to or change them, and upload them to eBay when you want to open your auction.

- Decide if you want to go auction, fixed-price, or Marketplace. Check out eBay's advice on this because it depends on the type of item.

When you list:

- Run 10-day listings that start on Thursdays. This gets two weekends into your auction time frame. Ideally you want your auction to end Sunday evening EST.

- Use low starting bids if you expect a lot of bidding. If you think bidders will be few, start closer to your desired minimum price. Only use a reserve price on very expensive items.

- Offer free shipping and delivery confirmation. Factor these into your price.

- Have a clearly posted policy for returns and money-back guarantees.

- Be prepared to answer questions on the item, even if the questions are stupid. If it's something other buyers might wonder about, post your response publicly.

- NEVER bid on your own item to 'up the bid', even under a different account name. It's illegal and it can get you permanently banned from the site as well.

- Treat potential buyers the way you would like to be treated.

After the auction:

- Contact the winning bidder quickly & *always* send the item to the *address provided by eBay.*

- Avoid accepting personal checks and money orders, if you can. These are common ploys used by scammers to get your stuff for free.

- Once you receive payment, package well and ship quickly. Include a note of thanks, a business card, or anything else you can think of to make your buyer feel special and to encourage future sales.

- Pay your eBay fees!

- Leave honest feedback for your buyer.

- Learn about your tax liabilities for this income and keep good records.

- Keep your records organized and your listings current.

A few final words on making money on eBay … start small and don't quit your day job *yet*. Go through the process with a few items, learning from experience as you go. Build your knowledge base and discover if working eBay is right for you. Learn to be thrifty with your listing fees so they don't eat up your profits, and also learn how to price things effectively. There's really no substitute for experience, but you can learn to avoid the biggest pitfalls through the mistakes of others. Yep, there's that research again.

Best of luck in your eBay adventures! Go forth and and get started building that $5000 a month eBay income!

Conclusion

Thank you again for downloading this book!

I hope this book was able to help you to understand the many different ways that you can make good money through eBay. One or more of them may be just the right answer for you.

The next step is to start selling!

Finally, if you enjoyed this book, then I'd like to ask you for a favor, would you be kind enough to leave a review for this book on Amazon? It'd be greatly appreciated!

Click here to leave a review for this book on Amazon!

Thank you and good luck!

Check Out My Other Books

Below you'll find some of my other popular books that are popular on Amazon and Kindle as well. Simply click on the links below to check them out.

Etsy Business Success: How to make your first $1,000 on Etsy without spending a dime

SEO Basics: How to use Search Engine Optimization (SEO) to take your business to the next level of success

Social Media Marketing for Beginners: How to build a social media strategy that really works

Affiliate Marketing for Beginners: Simple, smart and proven strategies to make A LOT of money online, the easy way

If the links do not work, for whatever reason, you can simply search for these titles on the Amazon website to find them.

www.ingramcontent.com/pod-product-compliance
Lightning Source LLC
Chambersburg PA
CBHW070925180526
45168CB00005B/2153